Mandala
Chic Coloring Book

Copyright: Published in the United States by Rosanna Cardenas
Published January 2017
ISBN-13: 978-1542651400
ISBN-10: 1542651409

All rights reserved. No part of this publication may be reproduced, stored in retrieval system, copied in any form or by any means, electronic, mechanical, photocopying, recording or otherwise transmitted without written permission from the publisher. Please do not participate in or encourage piracy of this material in any way. You must not circulate this book in any format. **Rosanna Cardenas** *does not control or direct users' actions and is not responsible for the information or content shared, harm and/or actions of the book readers.*

Thank you

www.ingramcontent.com/pod-product-compliance
Lightning Source LLC
Chambersburg PA
CBHW081115180526
45170CB00008B/2852